PONDER PAGES

Use this as you wish, but seek the gift of wonder:
a waste of time to read, but not a waste to ponder.

The Nicene Creed	2
Who Is Jesus Christ?	4
A Four-Page Course on the Bible	6
Bible Leaders	10
An Ancient Ritual	11
Church: The People of God	12
The Nature of the Sacred Liturgy	18
Our Year of Liturgy	19
The Temporal Cycle (The Seasons)	20
Sacraments	24
Paschal Mystery	28
Eucharist	29
Order of Mass	32
Reconciliation - Confession - Penance	35
An Examination of Conscience	38
Precepts of the Church	39
Forgiveness	40
Conversion - Transformation - Metanoia	41
Suffering & Death	42
Seeking to Understand Death	45

Copyright □ 2016 Stephen Joseph Wolf
All rights reserved. No part of this book may be copied or reproduced in any
form or by any means, except for the inclusion of brief quotations in a review,
without the written permission of the publisher.
idjc press   ISBN 978-1-937081-45-4   idjc.org

The NICENE CREED

1. One God
2. Two natures of Jesus - fully divine, and
   - fully human
3. Three divine Persons

I believe in one God,
the <u>Father</u> almighty,
maker of heaven and earth,
of all things visible and invisible.

4 lines are devoted to the Father.

I believe in one Lord Jesus Christ,
the Only Begotten <u>Son of God</u>,
born of the Father before all ages.
God from God, Light from Light,
true God from true God,
<u>begotten, not made</u>,
consubstantial with the Father;
through him all things were made.
For us men and for our salvation
he came down from heaven,
and by the Holy Spirit
was <u>incarnate</u> of the Virgin Mary,
and became man.

In the beginning was the Word, and the Word was with God, and the Word was God.
    - John 1:1

20 lines are devoted to the "Son."

For our sake he was <u>crucified</u>
under Pontius Pilate,
he <u>suffered death</u> and was <u>buried</u>,
and <u>rose</u> again on the third day
in accordance with the Scriptures.
He ascended into heaven
and is seated at the right hand of the Father.
He will come again in glory
to judge the living and the dead
and his kingdom will have no end.

See the First Letter to the Corinthians 15, perhaps our oldest creed.

I believe in the Holy Spirit,
the Lord, the <u>giver of life</u>,
who proceeds from the Father and the Son,
who with the Father and the Son
is adored and glorified,
who has <u>spoken</u> through the prophets.

4 lines are devoted to the Holy Spirit.

I believe in
<u>one</u>, <u>holy</u>, <u>catholic</u>
and <u>apostolic</u> Church.
I confess one Baptism
for the forgiveness of sins
and I look forward
to the <u>resurrection</u> of the dead
and the life of the world to come. Amen.

<u>Marks of the Church</u>
- **one**, only one, unity
- **holy**, set apart, bride of Christ, temple of the Holy Spirit
- **catholic**, "universal," unity & diversity
- **apostolic**, Tradition handed on from the Apostles

WHO IS JESUS CHRIST?

(1) Jesus of Nazareth was born into a first-century Jewish culture in the far eastern edge of the expansive Roman Empire. He lived, carried out his religious mission, and died in that time and place.

(2) The Resurrection of Jesus: His disciples believed and proclaimed that he was "raised" to a glorified life by the power of the God of Israel and exalted to a victorious union with God. Why did they say that?

(3) Incarnation: The Church came to confess Jesus Christ as the unexpected unique presence of God on earth. In Jesus, God became human like us, and in Jesus, the fullness of God's mystery is revealed.

(4) For Our Salvation: The Church also came to believe that the reason for this divine action is the pure love of God for all humanity and creation. God desires is that "everyone to be saved" (1st Timothy 2:4).

(5) Jesus Christ as the Fullness of True Humanity: The life of Jesus plunges us into the full mystery of our humanness, calling us to explore what it means to live a good human life in the most profound sense of the phrase, by looking at the life of Jesus.

(6) Continuing Presence of Christ: Catholic Christians believe that Jesus has not left his followers to walk this earthly way alone and unaided. He continues to strengthen and grace those who believe in him with his unique sanctifying presence, in many ways, above all in the sacraments, especially in the Eucharist.

(7) Lord of the Future: Jesus Christ directs creation to its fulfillment. We are not nomads; we are pilgrims with a destination. The vocation of each of us is to be a saint.

A brief summary from an excellent book:
Christology: True God, True Man, by Matthias Neuman, O.S.B.,
of *Catholic Basics: A Pastoral Ministry Series,*
Chicago: Loyola Press, 2002, 109 pages

A FOUR-PAGE COURSE on the BIBLE

CREATION
The beginning is a good place to begin,
the old, old stories on the beginnings:

THE CREATION	Genesis 1 & 2 (chapters 1 & 2)
	compare with Job 38 & Ps. 104
HUMAN SIN	Genesis 3; 4:1-13
NOAH	Genesis, chapters 6 to 8
TOWER OF BABEL	Genesis 11:1-9

PATRIARCHS
Chosen by God in the Covenant and the Exodus deliverance:

ABRAHAM	Genesis 12; 13; 21:1-5; 22:1-18
ISAAC	Genesis 24; 26:17-33
JACOB	Gen 27:1-45; 28:10-22; 32; 33
JOSEPH	Genesis 37; 41:1□ 46:7
MOSES	Exodus 1:6-14; 3:1-12; 5:1□ 6:8;
	7:1□ 20:21; 24:1□ 25:9; 35; 40;
	Numbers 3:1-10; 13:1□ 14:24;
	26:1-2,63-65
JOSHUA	Joshua chs. 1 to 4; 22 to 24

JUDGES
When, under Joshua's leadership, the Children of Israel had again conquered the Land of Canaan, they were advised in peace and in war by wise men and women known as "judges." Here are stories about some of them:

DEBORAH	Judges, chapter 4
GIDEON	Judges, chapters 6 to 8
SAMUEL	1 Samuel, chapters 1 to 3; 8

KINGS

After the people demanded and were given a king, they had a long succession of good and bad rulers. The Bible does not tell all about each one, but it does tell what kind of king each one was in words similar to 2 Kings 15:3 and 2 Kings 14:24. Here are some stories of a very few of the kings:

SAUL 1 Samuel chs. 9 to 12; 14; 31
DAVID 1 Samuel, chapters 16 to 20; 25;
2 Samuel 5:1-12; 6:1-15; chs. 7; 9; 11; 12; 21 to 24
1 Kings 2:1-10
SOLOMON 1 Kings 2:12; 3; 5; 6; 8:1-21
REHOBOAM & JEROBOAM 1 Kings 12; 15:1-6,25-30
AHAB 1 Kings 16:29-33; 21; 22:34-40
HEZEKIAH 2 Kings chs. 18 to 20
JOSIAH 2 Kings 22:1□ 23:28

PROPHETS

When the kings forgot God's will, prophets reminded them of it, even at the risk of their lives, here are some examples:

ELIJAH 1 Kings, chapters 17 to 19
2 Kings, chapters 1 & 2
ELISHA 2 Kings 2:1□ 13:20
MICAH 1 Kings, chapter 22

Listen to some of these prophets as they speak, most often in books bearing their names:

NEHEMIAH 1:1□ 7:3; ch. 8
ISAIAH 40:27-31
JEREMIAH 10:23-24
EZEKIEL 34:11-16
HOSEA ch. 11
HABAKKUK 3:19
ZEPHANIAH 3:9
HAGGAI 2:6-9
JOEL 2:21-25
AMOS 5:14-15
OBADIAH verse 15
MICAH 6:8
NAHUM 1:3,5-7
ZECHARIAH 7:8-14
MALACHI 2:10; 3:1-3

EXILE & RETURN

After Jerusalem had been destroyed and its people taken as captives to Babylon, they were at last allowed to go back to rebuild their homes and the Temple under capable leaders. Other people, inspired by God, added to the story.
They were singers, wise people, and storytellers:

SONGS	Psalms 1; 8; 19; 23; 24; 65; 67; 100; 103; 119:97-104; 121; 148; 150
	Song of Songs 2:8-13
SAYINGS	Proverbs 10:12; 11:28; 12:22; 15:1; 17:22; 19:17; 22:1; 26:27; 31:10,28
	Ecclesiastes 12:1-8, 13-14
	Wisdom 9:1-11
STORIES	Book of Esther; Book of Ruth; Book of Jonah; Job chs. 1; 2; 42
	Daniel, chapters 1; 3; 6;

JESUS OF NAZARETH

Sometimes the prophets spoke of a coming Messiah, God's own King. For his story, turn to the gospel accounts:

☐ MATTHEW   ☐ LUKE

☐ MARK   ☐ JOHN

THE TWELVE APOSTLES

After the crucifixion and resurrection of Jesus, his followers began to carry out his last command:

MATTHEW 28:19-20   MARK 16:15

You can read much of their story in:

THE ACTS OF THE APOSTLES
often referred to as The Book of Acts

PAUL

As the story of Jesus was spread abroad, first by his friends and followers, then by Paul, and later by other believers, letters of instruction and encouragement went from church to church. Here are some parts of these letters:

ROMANS ch. 8; 10:12-15	1 TIMOTHY 4:12
1 CORINTHIANS, chapter 13	2 TIMOTHY 2:15
GALATIANS 5:14, 22, 23	TITUS 3:8
EPHESIANS 6:1-4, 13-17	HEBREWS 13:2
PHILIPPIANS 4:8	JAMES 1:22-25; 3:7-8
COLOSSIANS 3:12-17	1 PETER 3:10-12
1 THESSALONIANS 4:13-18	1 JOHN 4:7-8

REVELATION

In a time of great suffering, one of the friends of Jesus wrote to Christians who faced torture and death that he might encourage them. He told them of a vision he had had of God's kingdom.   REVELATION chapter 21

These scripture references are chiefly from
A Promise to Keep by James D. Smart, The Westminster Press

LIVING TRADITION

The Church's liturgy has retained certain elements of the worship of the Old Covenant...notably:

- reading the Old Testament;
- praying the Psalms;
- above all, recalling the saving events and significant realities which have found their fulfillment in the mystery of Christ:

    - **Promise & Covenant**   **Kingdom & Temple**
    - **Exodus & Passover**   **Exile & Return**

CCC 1093

BIBLE LEADERS

These dates are guesses from various sources.

Patriarchs   Abraham & Sarah, Isaac & Rebekah,
(1850-1300 BC?)   Jacob (called Israel) & Rachel, Joseph

Exodus   Moses
(1300-1250 BC?)

Settlement in Canaan   Joshua, the Judges, Samuel
(1250-1130 BC?)

Rise of the Monarchy   Samuel, Saul, David, Solomon
(1020-922 BC?)

Divided Kingdom	Northern	Southern
(922-587 BC)	Jeroboam, Omri	Rehoboam
	Ahab & Jezebel & Elijah	
	Jehu, Jeroboam II & Amos	Uzziah & Hosea
		Hezekiah & Isaiah
		& Josiah

Return from Exile   Zerubbabel, Nehemiah, Ezra
(539 BC)

Alexander the Great & Hellenism
(332-39 BC)   Mattathias & Judas "the Maccabee"

Roman Rule	Herod the Great	**Jesus of Nazareth**
(39 BC - AD 100)		(born about 4 BC)
	Herod Antipas	
(about 30 AD)	& Pontius Pilate	Crucifixion & Resurrection

An ANCIENT RITUAL

And on the day named after the sun, all who live in city or countryside assemble, and the memoirs of the apostles or writings of the prophets are read for as long as time allows. When the lector has finished, the president addresses us, admonishing us and exhorting us to imitate the splendid things we have heard. Then we stand and pray, and as we said earlier, when we have finished praying, bread, wine, and water are brought up. The president offers prayer of thanksgiving, according to his ability, and the people give their assent with an "Amen!" Next, the gifts over which the thanksgiving has been spoken are distributed, and each one shares in them, while they are also sent via the deacon to the absent brothers and sisters.

The wealthy who are willing make contributions, each as he pleases, and the collection is deposited with the president, who aids orphans and widows, those who are in want because of sickness or other cause, those in prison, and visiting strangers; in short, he takes care of all in need.

The reason why we assemble on Sunday is that it is the first day: the day on which God…created the world, and the day on which Jesus Christ our Savior rose from the dead…

Saint Justin Martyr, 150 AD

CHURCH
The PEOPLE of GOD

All are called to the catholic unity of the people of God which prefigures and promotes universal peace. And to it belong, or are related in different ways:
- the catholic faithful,
- others who believe in Christ,
- [others who believe in the one God,]
- and all of humankind,
  called by God's grace to salvation.

The Catholic Faithful

Relying on scripture and tradition, the Second Vatican Council teaches that this pilgrim church is required for salvation. Present to us in his body which is the church, Christ alone is mediator and the way of salvation. He expressly asserted the necessity of faith and Baptism (see Mark 16:16; John 3:5) and thereby affirmed at the same time the necessity of the church, which people enter through Baptism as through a door. Therefore, those could not be saved who refuse either to enter the church, or to remain in it, while knowing that it was founded by God through Christ as required for salvation.

Fully incorporated into the society of the church are those who, possessing the Spirit of Christ, accept its entire structure and all the means of salvation established within it and who in its visible structures are united with Christ, who rules it through the Supreme Pontiff and the bishops, by the bonds of profession of faith, the sacraments, ecclesiastical government, and communion.

A person who does not persevere in charity, however, is not saved, even though incorporated into the church. Such people remain indeed in the bosom of the church, but only "bodily" not "in their hearts" (Saint Augustine). All daughters and sons of the church should nevertheless remember that their exalted status is not to be ascribed to their own merits, but to the special grace of Christ.

Others Who Believe in Christ

The Church has many reasons for knowing that it is joined to the baptized who are honored by the name of Christian, but do not profess the faith in its entirety or have not preserved unity of communion under the successor of Peter.

For there are many who hold sacred scripture in honor as a rule of faith and of life, who display a sincere religious zeal, who lovingly believe in God the Father Almighty and in Christ, the Son of God and the Saviour. They are sealed by Baptism which unites them to Christ and they recognize and accept other sacraments in their own churches or ecclesiastical communities.

There is furthermore a communion in prayer and other spiritual benefits. Indeed, there is a true union in the holy Spirit for, by his gifts and graces, his sanctifying power is active in them also and he has strengthened some of them even to the shedding of their blood.

And so the Spirit stirs up desires and actions in all of Christ's disciples in order that all may be peacefully united, as Christ ordained, in one flock under one shepherd. Mother church never ceases to pray, hope and work that this may be achieved, and she exhorts her children to purification and renewal so that the sign of Christ may shine more brightly over the face of the church.

Others Who Believe in the One God

Those who have not yet accepted the Gospel are related to the people of God in various ways.

There is, first, that people (the Jews) to whom the covenants and promises were made, and from whom Christ was born in the flesh (see Romans 9:4-5), a people in virtue of their election beloved for the sake of the fathers, for God never regret his gifts or his call (see Romans 11:28-39).

But the plan of salvation also includes those who acknowledge the Creator, first among whom are the Moslems: they profess to hold the faith of Abraham, and together with us they adore the one, merciful God, who will judge humanity on the last day.

Others Called by God's Grace to Salvation

Nor is God remote from those who in shadows and images seek the unknown God, since he gives to everyone life and breath and all things (see Acts 17:25-28) and since the Savior wills everyone to be saved (see 1 Timothy 2:4).

Those who, through no fault of their own, do not know the Gospel of Christ or his church, but who nevertheless seek God with a sincere heart, and, moved by grace, try in their actions to do his will as they know it through the dictates of their conscience — these too may attain eternal salvation.

Nor will divine providence deny the assistance necessary for salvation to those who, without any fault of theirs, have not yet arrived at an explicit knowledge of God, and who, not without grace, strive to lead a good life. Whatever of good or truth is found amongst them is considered by the church to be a preparation for the Gospel and given by him who enlightens all men and women that they may at length have life.

Missionaries to the Un-churched

But very often, deceived by the Evil One, people have lost their way in their thinking, have exchanged the truth of God for a lie and served the creature rather than the Creator (see Romans 1:21 and 25). Or else, living and dying in this world without God, they are exposed to ultimate despair. This is why, to procure the glory of God and the salvation of all of these people, the church, mindful of the Lord's command, "preach the Gospel to every creature" (Mark 16:15), takes great care to encourage the missions.

Vatican Council II:
Dogmatic Constitution on the Church
(Lumen Gentium) 1964,
from paragraphs 13-16

The NATURE of the SACRED LITURGY

Christ is always present in his church, especially in liturgical celebrations.

He is present in the sacrifice of the Mass both in the person of his minister, "the same now offering, through the ministry of priests, who formerly offered himself on the cross," and most of all in the eucharistic species.

By his power he is present in the sacraments so that when anybody baptizes it is really Christ himself who baptizes.

He is present in his word since it is he himself who speaks when the holy scriptures are read in church.

Lastly, he is present when the church prays and sings, for he has promised "where two or three are gathered together in my name there am I in the midst of them" (Matthew 18:20).

Vatican Council II: *The Constitution on the Sacred Liturgy (Sacrosanctum Concilium)* 1963, from paragraph 7

OUR YEAR of LITURGY

Time is a fundamental part of creation.

Sacred time is around the person of Jesus Christ.

The LORD'S DAY
Sunday; 1st day of the week; the 8th day; 1st of all holy days.

ORDERING of OTHER DAYS
solemnity > feast > obligatory memorial > optional memorial

OCTAVES
The "eight days" of Easter and the "eight days" of Christmas can be called the pillars, or hinges, of the liturgical year.

Sanctoral Cycle (January 1 to December 31)
"the Proper of Saints"

Mary, the martyrs, and the other saints, holy men and women who are models of gospel living, are remembered each year on their anniversaries. These celebrations remind us of the centrality of the mysteries of Christ in their lives. Most saints are remembered on or near the date of their earthly deaths and births to eternal life.

The TEMPORAL CYCLE (The Seasons)

ADVENT — *joyful expectancy & hope*
color: Violet — *penance is secondary*

Advent begins the liturgical year on the fourth Sunday before Christmas. As a practical matter, the first Sunday of Advent is the Sunday nearest to November 30, the feast of St. Andrew. Advent is a time of waiting and longing for the coming of the Messiah who has come, and for a new spiritual birth. A season of hope as well as penance, Advent explores the writings of the Old Testament prophets in the Mass readings.

CHRISTMAS — *joy of the Birth of the Messiah*
color: White — *Incarnation: Word made flesh*

Christmas begins with Christmas Day, goes through Epiphany, and concludes with the Baptism of the Lord. Although we do not know the exact date of the birth of Jesus, it is celebrated every year on the 25th of December, three days or so after the Winter solstice, the shortest day of sunlight in the year. With the Incarnation, light overcomes darkness. Related feasts are the Annunciation on March 25 (nine months prior) and the birth of John the Baptist (six months prior). By his Incarnation, Christ has taken on human form as both fully human and fully God.

> ◻◻◻◻◻◻◻◻◻◻◻◻
> *In each year, up to ten weeks of **Ordinary Time** is sandwiched between the seasons of Christmas and Lent.*
> ◻◻◻◻◻◻◻◻◻◻◻◻

LENT *- prayer, fasting & almsgiving*
color: Violet *- union with Jesus' suffering*
  - sacrifice, penance & service

Lent is sometimes described as the "Church on retreat." The 40 days of Lent are patterned after the 40 days spent by Jesus in his desert temptation and the 40 years of wilderness wandering of the Chosen People. The season begins on Ash Wednesday and ends on Holy Thursday. Something about Lent (the word means *springtime*) seems to capture our shared ritual imagination. Prayer, fasting and giving of alms help to focus Lent as a time to reflect on how well we are living our Baptism.

TRIDUUM *- one "3 day" liturgy*
colors: White & Red

Meaning "three days," the Triduum celebrates Easter. The Paschal Triduum begins with the Mass of the Lord's Supper on Holy Thursday. Part of this celebration is the washing of the feet of people in the community by a bishop or a priest. On Good Friday, a gospel narrative of the passion of Christ is read, and the cross is venerated by the people. At the Easter Vigil, baptisms and rites of full communion are celebrated with those coming into the Church through the Rite of Christian Initiation of Adults (R.C.I.A.) and for children above age 7 entering the Church. The Easter Vigil is called the "mother of all liturgies." Baptisms of infants may be celebrated at Easter Sunday morning Masses, and the single liturgy of the three day Triduum concludes on Easter Sunday evening.

EASTER *- joy of the resurrection*
color: White

"Easter" is a Sunday (the first of all Sundays), an Octave (the eight days of Easter), and a season that concludes on Pentecost Sunday. Tied to the ancient Jewish celebration of Passover, Easter is the first Sunday following the first full moon after the Spring (*vernal*) equinox. The lighted Easter Candle kept near the Ambo is a reminder that through his actions and word Christ is the light of the world. During the 50 days of Easter, the Church reflects on the mystery of our Redemption through the *Paschal Mystery*: the saving death and resurrection of Jesus.

PENTECOST — *coming of the Holy Spirit*
color: Red

On Pentecost Sunday, the "50th day" of Easter, we celebrate the Holy Spirit, the flame of God's love. The New Testament events are the coming of the Holy Spirit to the disciples in the upper room and the commission to preach and evangelize all nations.

ORDINARY TIME — *hope; presence of Christ*
color: Green

Ordinary Time comes in two sections. The first is between the Christmas season and Lent. The second is between Pentecost and the following Advent. During these 33 or 34 "neutral weeks," the fullness of Christ's mystery is celebrated in all its aspects, as well as the presence of Christ in his Church. The Solemnity of Christ the King is the last Sunday of Ordinary Time and the beginning of the last week of the liturgical year.

SACRAMENTS

…efficacious signs of grace,
instituted by Christ
and entrusted to the Church,
by which divine life
is dispensed to us…

SACRAMENTS of INITIATION
1. **Baptism**
2. **Confirmation**
3. **Eucharist**

The visible rites
by which the sacraments are celebrated
signify and make present
the graces proper to each sacrament.

SACRAMENTS of HEALING
1. **Reconciliation**
2. **Anointing of the Sick**

They bear fruit in those
who receive them with
the required dispositions.

Church celebrates the sacraments
as a priestly community
structured by
the baptismal priesthood
and the priesthood of ordained ministers.

The Holy Spirit
prepares the faithful for the sacraments
by the Word of God
and the faith which welcomes that word
in well-disposed hearts.

Thus the sacraments
strengthen faith
and express it.

SACRAMENTS of COMMUNION
1. **Marriage**
2. **Ordination**

Catechism of the Catholic Church, 2nd Edition # 1131-33

The SACRAMENTS . . .

...are perceptible signs (words & actions)
accessible to our human nature. (senses, mind, etc.)
By the action of Christ and the power of
the Holy Spirit they make present efficaciously
the grace they signify.

CCC 1084

...have a threefold purpose:
1. to sanctify humanity,
2. to build up the Body of Christ, and
3. to give worship to God.

Because they are signs they also instruct...
...they nourish, strengthen, and express faith.

CCC 1123

...are "efficacious" because in them Christ himself is
at work; it is Christ who baptizes, Christ who acts
in his sacraments in order to communicate
the grace that each sacrament signifies.

CCC 1127

...are "of the Church" in a double sense:
- The Church is the sacrament of Christ's action
  at work in her through the mission of the
  Holy Spirit.
- "The sacraments make the Church," since they
  manifest and communicate to humanity, above all
  in the Eucharist, the mystery of communion with
  God who is love, One in three persons.

Sts. Augustine & Aquinas, CCC 1118

The SACRAMENTS . . .

...act *ex opere operato*   (literally:)
"by the very fact of the action being performed."
They act by virtue of the saving work of Christ,
accomplished once for all.   Council of Trent, 1547
CCC 1128

...are "the masterworks of God"...

CCC 1116

By the mid 1100's AD, it was becoming common in the Church to speak of seven sacraments, perhaps suggested first by Peter Lombard (d. 1160). Saint Thomas Aquinas (d. 1274) accepted them, as did the Council of Florence in 1439.

Anthony Gilles, People of God:
The History of Catholic Christianity,
St. Anthony Messenger Press, 2000, pg. 74

Tertullian (d.ca.220), a lawyer from North Africa, was the first to translate the greek word "mysterion" (used to name any manifestation of God's power and love in space and time) into Latin as "sacramentum." A "sacramentum" was the "pledge" or "oath" a soldier made upon entering military service. Sometimes this oath was accompanied by branding the new soldier on the arm with a sign of the general he was to serve.

Mark R. Francis, The Harper Collins
Encyclopedia of Catholicism, 1995, pg. 1146

Three sacraments confer, in addition to grace, a sacramental character or "seal" which is indelible and remains for ever in the Christian, the three which cannot be repeated:

   1. Baptism   2. Confirmation   3. Holy Orders

As fire transforms into itself everything it touches, so the Holy Spirit transforms into the divine life whatever is subjected to his power.

CCC 1127

A SACRAMENT . . .

…"is not wrought by righteousness of either the celebrant or the recipient, but by the power of God."

St. Thomas Aquinas, CCC 1128

…is a sign that
- commemorates what precedes it (Christ's Passion)
- demonstrates what is accomplished in us through Christ's Passion   (grace)
- and prefigures what that Passion pledges to us.   (future glory.)

St. Thomas Aquinas, CCC 1130

lex orandi, lex credenda
"The law of prayer is the law of faith."
(As we pray, so we believe.)

Liturgy is a constitutive element
of the holy and living Tradition.

Prosper of Aquitaine, 5th century, Dei Verbum 8, CCC 1124

PASCHAL MYSTERY

Christ's Work in the Liturgy: CCC 1084ff.

**Christ glorified
from the time of the Church of the Apostles
is present in the earthly liturgy
which participates in the liturgy of heaven.**

Christ's Paschal mystery is a real event that occurred in our history, but it is unique: all other historical events happen once, and then they pass away, swallowed up in the past. The Paschal mystery of Christ, by contrast, cannot remain only in the past, because by his death he destroyed death, and all that Christ is □ all that he did and suffered for people □ participates in the divine eternity, and so transcends all times while being made present in them all. The event of the Cross and Resurrection *abides* and draws everything toward life.

CCC 1085

In the earthly liturgy we share in a foretaste of that heavenly liturgy which is celebrated in the Holy City of Jerusalem toward which we journey as pilgrims, where Christ is sitting at the right hand of God, Minister of the sanctuary and of the true tabernacle.

SC 8, cf. LG 50, CCC 1090

EUCHARIST

The Eucharist . . .

…is the "source and summit of the Christian life."
LG 11, CCC 1324

> All our endeavors, prayers and activities
> move toward the celebration of the Eucharist
> and flow from it. IHL 203

…completes Christian initiation. CCC 1322

> Baptism ☐ ☐ Confirmation ☐ ☐ Eucharist

…identifies the Church:

> The Eucharist is the efficacious sign and sublime
> cause of that communion in the divine life and
> that unity of the People of God by which
> the Church is kept in being. EM 6, CCC 1325

…signifies the already and the not yet:

> By the Eucharistic celebration we "already"
> unite ourselves with the heavenly liturgy
> and "anticipate" eternal life, when God will be
> all in all. 1 Corinthians 15:28, CCC 1326

…is the sum and summary of our faith:

> Our way of thinking is attuned to the Eucharist,
> and the Eucharist in turn confirms our way of
> thinking. St. Irenaeus, CCC 1327

For more on the Eucharist see CCC paragraphs 1322-1419.

EUCHARIST	The word means "thanksgiving," from the Greek: *eucharistein* and *eulogein*.
THE LORD'S SUPPER	Connected with the supper which the Lord took with his disciples. Anticipates the wedding feast of the Lamb in the heavenly Jerusalem.
THE BREAKING OF BREAD	...as Jesus did at the Lord's Supper after his Resurrection. How first Christians designated their Eucharistic assemblies. Acts 2:42, 46; 20:7, 11
EUCHARISTIC ASSEMBLY (synaxis)	The Eucharist is celebrated amid the assembly of the faithful which is the visible expression of the Church. 1 Corinthians 11:17-34
MEMORIAL	...of the Lord's Passion and Resurrection, remembering that makes the event present.
THE HOLY SACRIFICE	The Eucharist makes present the one sacrifice of Christ the Savior and includes the Church's offering.

(Also: HOLY SACRIFICE OF THE MASS, "SACRIFICE OF PRAISE," SPIRITUAL SACRIFICE, PURE AND HOLY SACRIFICE)

THE HOLY AND DIVINE LITURGY	The Church's whole liturgy finds its center and most intense expression in the celebration of this sacrament. (Also: THE SACRED MYSTERIES)
MOST BLESSED SACRAMENT	The Eucharist is the Sacrament of sacraments. The Eucharist reserved in the tabernacle to be taken to the sick is called the Blessed Sacrament.
HOLY COMMUNION	By the Eucharist, we unite ourselves to Christ, who makes us sharers in his Body & Blood to form a single body.

(Also: THE HOLY THINGS, BREAD OF ANGELS, BREAD FROM HEAVEN, VIATICUM...)

HOLY MASS (MISSA)	The liturgy concludes with the sending forth (*missio*) of the faithful, so that we may fulfill God's will in our daily lives.

The Last Supper: Mt 26:17-30, Mk 14:12-26, Lk 22:7-20
The Bread of Life Discourse: John 6:22-69

How holy this feast in which Christ is our food; his passion is recalled; grace fills our hearts; and we receive a pledge of the glory to come, alleluia.
Evening Prayer antiphon for Corpus Christi, attributed to St. Thomas Aquinas

ORDER of MASS

INTRODUCTORY RITES

Entrance Chant Veneration of the Altar, at a central position
Presider Chair
Sign of the Cross

Penitential Act Forgiveness and praise, celebration of God's mercy.

Gloria on Sundays, Solemnities, and Feasts

Collect Prayer of the Universal Church

LITURGY OF THE WORD

From the 1st Century Jewish Synagogue Service?
(three year repeating cycle of lectionary readings)

Old Testament Reading Some connection to the Gospel reading, or from the Acts of the Apostles in the Easter season.

Responsorial Psalm A response to the Old Testament reading.

New Testament Reading From a Letter (epistle) or Revelation.

Gospel Reading The "Good News" (*Evangelion*) of the life, ministry, preaching, healing, suffering, death, and resurrection of Jesus Christ.

Homily	Directed toward entering more deeply into mystery, forming for witness in the world, anamnesis, symbols, participation, praise, leading naturally to the table
Profession of Faith	Niceno-Constantinopolitan Creed, from 325 AD, or the Apostles' Creed, Roman baptismal Symbol.
Prayer of the Faithful	Particular needs of all people throughout the world; also called the Universal Prayer.

LITURGY OF THE EUCHARIST

Connected to the 1st Century Jewish Passover and the Sacrificial Liturgy of the Jerusalem Temple?

Preparation of the Gifts	bread, wine, water, (and collection) Bridge between Word & Eucharist, washing of hands; concludes with the Prayer over the Offerings.

Eucharistic Prayer *Gospel links?*
  I. Roman Canon *(Matthew)*
     a noble simplicity, the Church of the Messiah
 II. Apostolic Tradition of Hippolytus *(Mark)*
     strong Son of God conquering powers of darkness
III. Vatican II, based on Mazarabic Tradition *(Luke)*
     people of God, a pilgrim people
 IV. Probably used by St. Basil the Great *(John)*
     the Holy Spirit, Christ loving his own to the end

Lord's Prayer　　　　　　Lord, teach us how to pray.

Rite of Peace　Liturgical greeting among Christians,
　　　　　　a sign of neighborly love and unity.

Breaking of Bread　　　　*Lamb of God…*
　　　　Lamb of God…　Lamb of God…
　May this mingling of the Body and Blood of our Lord
　　Jesus Christ bring eternal life to us who receive it.
　　　　　Behold the Lamb of God…

Communion　　　　　　procession
　　　Bread and wine, one bowl and one cup,
　　　common life in the Lord through baptism,
　　　membership in the one Body of Christ.

Prayer after　　　　After silence, concludes
　Communion　　　　the Liturgy of the Eucharist.

CONCLUDING RITES

Blessing　　　　"A liturgical expression
　　　　　　of God's generosity and love."

Dismissal　　　　Each member of the congregation
　　　　　　is sent to do good works,
　　　　　　praising and blessing the Lord.

HOLY MASS:　　　　(MISSA)
The liturgy concludes with the
sending forth (*missio*) of the faithful,
so that we may fulfill God's will in our daily lives.

RECONCILIATION – CONFESSION – PENANCE

Go and learn the meaning of the words,
"I desire mercy, not sacrifice."
I did not come to call the righteous, but sinners.

Jesus of Nazareth
Matthew 9:13

Sin is . . .

...an abuse of the freedom given to us by God
that we may freely love God and one another.

...an offense against God.

...a rupture of communion with God.

...not the same thing as temptation;
even Christ was tempted in the desert.

...can be an action, thought, inaction, omission...

...when a thing is wrong,
and I know it is wrong,
and I freely do the thing anyway.

The Sacrament of Reconciliation:

1. Examination of Conscience *How am I distant from God?*

2. Confession *This I Have Done.*

3. Accepting a Penance *Yes, This I Will Do.*

4. Contrition *Lord, I Am Sorry...*

5. Absolution *The Prayer of the Church.*

6. Doing the Penance *Toward Amendment of Life.*

CONFESSION	Disclosure of sins to a priest

*Whoever confesses his or her sins
...is already working with God...
The beginning of good works is the
confession of evil works. You do the
truth and come to the light.* — Saint Augustine

SATISFACTION or RESTITUTION	Doing what is possible to repair the harm:

> *Absolution takes away sin,
> but it does not remedy all
> the disorders sin has caused.*
> — Council of Trent (1551)

PENANCE	- imposed by the confessor
	- accepted & performed by the penitent
PENANCES (examples)	scripture, prayer, fasting, giving alms, works of mercy, reaching out, seeking and defending justice, enduring persecution, admitting faults, every sincere act of worship, concern for the poor "fraternal correction," pilgrimages
CONTRITION	Sorrow of the soul, detesting the sin committed and resolving to not sin again.

PERFECT: from loving God above all
IMPERFECT: also a gift from God

FORGIVENESS By the sacramental absolution God grants "pardon and peace."

CONVERSION Baptism is the principal place for the first and fundamental conversion. It is by faith in the Gospel and by Baptism that one renounces evil and gains salvation, that is, the forgiveness of all sins and the gift of new life. CCC 1427

CONCUPISCENCE, The inclination to sin: The new life in Christian initiation has not abolished the frailty and weakness of human nature ...
This is the struggle of conversion... CCC 1426

SECOND CONVERSION Christ's call to conversion continues... This endeavor is not just a human work. It is the movement of a "contrite heart," drawn and moved by the grace to respond to the merciful love of God who loved us first.
(Psalms 51:17, John 6:44; 12:32, 1 John 4:10)

In the Church there are water and tears:
- the water of Baptism, and
- the tears of repentance. St. Ambrose

RECONCILIATION Imparts to the sinner the life of God who reconciles.

For more on Reconciliation see CCC paragraphs 1420-98.

An EXAMINATION of CONSCIENCE

Following the example of the prodigal son, who "came to himself" (Luke 15:17), ponder your life by the light of the Gospel and let the Holy Spirit show when you have acted contrary to the teaching of Jesus in thought, word or deed.   *World Youth Day 2002*

In Relation to God:
- ☐ Is my heart set on God, so that I really love God above all?
- ☐ Are private prayer and Sunday worship a priority?
- ☐ Have I love and reverence for the name of God?
- ☐ Am I hesitant or ashamed to witness to my faith in God?
- ☐ Am I making an effort to grow spiritually? How? When?
- ☐ How am I responding to my baptismal commitments to witness to Christ and to be a person of faith, hope and love?
- ☐ Do I turn to God only when I am in need?

In Relation to Others:
- ☐ Am I quick to forgive and slow to judge?
- ☐ Do I use others as a means to an end?
- ☐ Do I take care of the poor, sick and defenseless?
- ☐ Am I sincere and honest in my dealings with others?
- ☐ Have I been the cause of another's committing sin?
- ☐ Are any relationships causing me concern today?
- ☐ Do I care for and respect the environment in which I live?

In Relation to Myself:
- ☐ Do I truly live as a Christian and give a good example?
- ☐ Do I believe that I am made in the image of God?
- ☐ Am I too concerned about myself and my stuff?
- ☐ What do I spend most of my time thinking about?
- ☐ Have I kept my senses and my body pure and chaste as a temple of the Holy Spirit?
- ☐ Do I bear grudges; do I contemplate revenge?
- ☐ Do I seek to be humble and be an instrument of peace?

PRECEPTS of the CHURCH

The precepts of the Church are set in the context of a **moral life** bound to and nourished by **liturgical life**. [Their] obligatory character...is meant to guarantee to the faithful **the very necessary minimum** in the spirit of prayer and moral effort, in the growth in love of God and neighbor.　　　　　　　　　　　CCC 2041-43

1. **To <u>attend Mass</u> on Sundays and on holy days of obligation and <u>rest</u> from servile labor**: Sanctify the day commemorating the Resurrection of the Lord as well as the principal liturgical feasts honoring the mysteries of the Lord, the Blessed Virgin Mary, and the saints, in the first place by participating in the Eucharistic celebration, in which the Christian community is gathered, and by resting from those works and activities which could impede such a sanctification of these days.

2. **To <u>confess sins</u> at least once a year**: Prepare for the Eucharist by the reception of the sacrament of reconciliation which continues Baptism's work of conversion and forgiveness. [This precept becomes essential in cases of serious sin.]

3. **To receive the <u>sacrament of the Eucharist</u> at least during the <u>Easter</u> season**: This is the minimum reception of the Lord's Body and Blood in connection with the Paschal feasts, the origin and center of the Christian liturgy.

4. **To observe the days of <u>fasting</u> and <u>abstinence</u> established by the Church**: The times of ascesis and penance prepare us for the liturgical feasts, and they help us acquire mastery over our instincts and freedom of heart.

5. **To <u>help provide</u> for the needs of the Church**: The faithful are obliged to assist with the material needs of the Church, each according to his or her abilities.

FORGIVENESS

...AS WE FORGIVE THOSE WHO TRESPASS AGAINST US...

...It is impossible to keep the Lord's commandment by imitating the divine model from outside; there has to be a vital participation, coming from the depths of the heart, in the holiness and mercy and the love of our God. Only the Spirit by whom we live can make "ours" the same mind that was in Christ Jesus. Then the unity of forgiveness becomes possible and we find ourselves "forgiving one another, *as* God in Christ forgave" us. CCC 2842

It is..."in the depths of the *heart*" that everything is bound and loosed. It is not in our power not to feel or to forget an offense; but the heart that offers itself to the Holy Spirit turns injury into compassion and purifies the memory in transforming the hurt into intercession. CCC 2843

Christian prayer extends to the *forgiveness of enemies*, transfiguring the disciple by configuring him or her to the Master. Forgiveness is a high-point of Christian prayer; only hearts attuned to God's compassion can receive the gift of prayer. Forgiveness also bears witness that, in our world, love is stronger than sin. The martyrs of yesterday and today bear this witness to Jesus. Forgiveness is the fundamental condition of the reconciliation of the children of God with their Father and...with one another. CCC 2844

There is no limit or measure to this essentially divine forgiveness, whether one speaks of "sins" as in Luke (11:4), or "debts" as in Matthew (6:12). We are always debtors: "Owe no one anything, except to love one another" (Romans 13:8). The communion of the Holy Trinity is the source and criterion of truth in every relationship. It is lived out in prayer, above all in the Eucharist. CCC 2845

CONVERSION

TRANSFORMATION

METANOIA

See Luke 15:11-32

Try, if you please, to invent a different ending for this story. Make the old man rebuff the boy at first; have him stand on his dignity and require of the rascal proofs of his change of heart; let him read him a sermon on wild oats before the forgiving kiss is bestowed; have him take the penitent at his word – as he richly deserves to be taken – and try him out with the slaves for a year or two, till the family pride, or outraged justice, is satisfied. Imagine, in short, *any possible ending but this,* and you have destroyed the noblest picture of redeeming grace ever created, and lowered God to the level of human virtue. Heathen religions in plenty, and some versions of the Christian religion, furnish us with the alternatives suggested above, or worse; Christ alone shows us the suffering Father who saves by forgiving.

Interpretation by Dr. Albert Edward Bailey and the painting
DER VERLORENE SOHN (The Forlorn Son) by Eugene Burnand,
The Gospel in Art, pg. 173, Pilgrim Press, Boston, MA,
both from *Christ And The Fine Arts,* anthology by Cynthia Pearl Maus, Harper & Brothers Publishers, Copyright ☐ 1938, pgs 216-218. All rights reserved.

SUFFERING & DEATH

For we walk by faith, not by sight.
2 Corinthians 5:7

The world we live in often seems very far from the one promised us by faith. Our experiences of evil and suffering, injustice, and death, seem to contradict the Good News... It is then we...turn to the *witnesses of faith*: Abraham..., Mary..., and so many others.   CCC 164,165

Suffering . . .
...is part of the mystery of what it is to be human.
...has many forms: emotional, physical, spiritual, mental.
...is sometimes freely chosen as a form of self-discipline
   or as a necessary component of serving others.
...is sometimes caused by human error or lack of care.
...can be caused by sin, a consequence of human
   freedom.
...Some people choose to be so selfish that others suffer.
...can also happen with no apparent cause or purpose.
   Only by faith can people who endure these tragedies
   believe that "all things work for good for those who
   love God" and nothing "will be able to separate us
   from the love of God." (Romans 8:28,39)
...calls us to serve as Christ served those who suffered,
   and to serve them with the same devotion
   one would serve Christ himself.
   The Harper Collins Encyclopedia of Catholicism, and
   Leonard Foley, OFM, *Believing In Jesus*, pg. 76
...is found all through the Bible.

Death . . .

...IS THE END OF EARTHLY LIFE.

Our lives are measured by time, in the course of which we change, grow old and, as with all living beings on earth, death seems like the normal end of life.   CCC1007
Death is the end of a human's earthly pilgrimage.
When "the single course of our earthly life" is completed, we shall not return to other earthly lives: Lumen Gentium 48
"It is appointed for men to die once."   Hebrews 9:27
There is no "reincarnation" after death.   CCC 1013

...IS A CONSEQUENCE OF SIN.

Death entered the world on account of human sin.
   (Cf. Genesis 2:17, 3:3, 3:19; Wisdom 1:12; Romans 5:12, 6:23; DS 1511)
Even though human nature is mortal, God had destined man not to die. Death was therefore contrary to the plans of God the Creator...   Wisdom 1:13-14, 2:23-34
"Bodily death, from which man would have been immune had he not sinned" is thus "the last enemy" of humanity left to be conquered.   1 Corinth. 15:26, GS 18.2, CCC 1008

...IS TRANSFORMED BY CHRIST.

Jesus, the Son of God, also himself suffered the death that is part of the human condition. Yet, despite his anguish as he faced death, he accepted it in an act of complete & free submission to his Father's will.   Mark 14:33-34, Hebrews 5:7-8
The obedience of Jesus has transformed the curse of death into a blessing.   Romans 5:19-21, CCC 1009
The dying can participate in the death of the Lord, for those who die in Christ's grace, so too can they also share His Resurrection.   Romans 6:3-9, Philippians 3:10-11, ccc 1006

It is in the face of death that the riddle of human existence grows most acute.   Gaudium et Spes 18

Death . . .

…has positive meaning:
> "For to me to live is Christ, and to die is gain." Phil 1:21
> "The saying is sure: if we have died with him,
> we will also live with him." 2 Tim 2:11

…for the Christian has sacramentally already happened through Baptism . . . (and so) physical death completes this "dying with Christ." CCC 1010

…is (where, how) God calls us to himself. Therefore, the Christian can experience a desire for death like St. Paul's: "My desire is to depart and be with Christ." Phil 1:23

…can be how the Christian can transform his or her own death into an act of obedience and love towards the Father, after the example of Christ: CCC 1011
- My earthly desire has been crucified; …there is living water in me, water that murmurs and says within me: Come to the Father. St. Ignatius of Antioch
- I want to see God and, in order to see him, I must die. St. Teresa of Avila
- I am not dying; I am entering life. St. Therese of Lisieux

…lends urgency to our lives: Remembering our mortality helps us realize that we have only a limited time in which to bring our lives to fulfillment: CCC 1007
> *Remember also your Creator in the days of your youth,*
> *…before the dust returns to the earth as it was,*
> *and the spirit returns to God who gave it.* Ecclesiastes 12:1,7

Remember that you are dust, and to dust you shall return.
Prayer of Ash Wednesday from Genesis 3:19

Indeed for your faithful, Lord, life is changed not ended…
Eucharistic Prayer Preface I, Funeral Rite

SEEKING to UNDERSTAND DEATH

OLD TESTAMENT — *Sheol: Dwelling of the Shades*
The passage of the person from the land of the living to *sheol* (Hebrew), the dark, cheerless realm of the dead where there can be no happiness and no praise of God.

LATER OLD TESTAMENT — *Separation of Soul & Body*
Closer to the Greek philosophical notion of death as separation of soul and body,   Wisdom 3:1-5, 4:15
eternal life coming to be understood
not in terms of immortality of the soul
but in terms of the resurrection of the body.   Daniel 12:2

NEW TESTAMENT — *Overcome by Christ's Dying & Rising*
Adding the notions of
the enslaving consequences of sin   Romans 5:12, 6:23
and that power decisively overcome by the death and resurrection of Jesus.   Hebrews 2:14, 2 Timothy 1:10

CHRISTIAN TRADITION — *Consequence of Original Sin*
Though a consequence of original sin,   Council of Trent
death is a defining event in the life of the Christian:
In the face of death, one's essential disposition toward the mystery of God is disclosed as either an obedient and humble acknowledgment of one's finitude and dependence, or as a rebellious and ultimately self-defeating assertion of one's autonomy.   The Harper Collins Encyclopedia
of Catholicism, 1995, pg. 398

May the peace of God, which is beyond all understanding, keep our hearts and minds in the knowledge and love of God and of his Son, our Lord Jesus Christ. Amen.
From the Blessing of the Funeral Rite

www.ingramcontent.com/pod-product-compliance
Lightning Source LLC
Chambersburg PA
CBHW030202100526
44592CB00009B/408